How to Respond to . . .
THE NEW CHRISTIAN RELIGIONS

How to Respond to . . .

THE NEW CHRISTIAN RELIGIONS

Philip H. Lochhaas

Publishing House
St. Louis

THE RESPONSE SERIES

How to Respond to the Cults
How to Respond to Transcendental Meditation
How to Respond to the Lodge
How to Respond to the Latter Day Saints
How to Respond to the Occult
How to Respond to Jehovah's Witnesses
How to Respond to the Eastern Religions
How to Respond to the New Christian Religions

Concordia Publishing House, St. Louis, Missouri
Copyright © 1979 Concordia Publishing House
Manufactured in the United States of America

79 - 599

Foreword to the Response Series

The Gallup Opinion Index on Religion in America, 1977—78, says that the "search is on." People of all ages are searching for deeper meaning in their lives. "There is new evidence of considerable and growing spiritual experimentation, a new interest in the cults and mysticism." That is why the statistics indicate that one in eight Americans is engaged in some sort of experimental religion, which includes the cults, mysticism, and Eastern religions.

This "search" has spawned a continuing increase in the number of cults, sects, and new contemporary religion movements, and with this growth comes the need to help Christian people understand and respond. This need was first expressed by The Lutheran Church—Missouri Synod assembled in national convention at Anaheim, Calif., July 1975. In response to the request of that convention the Board for Evangelism developed "The Response Series," a series of booklets which include a foundation booklet dealing with *The Cults* and five booklets dealing with specific religious movements. These were first issued in 1977 and have been very popular both in The Lutheran Church—Missouri Synod and among other concerned Christians.

The series was planned so it would be expanded to include other groups than those covered in the first issue. It is now possible to add two more, *The "New 'Christian' Religions"* and *The Eastern Religions*. If the need and popularity of the series continues, other booklets will be added in the future.

The booklets are intended to be used in two ways. They can be read and studied by an individual who is confronted with a specific need to know more about one movement, or they can be studied by a Bible class or study group.

Most of the contemporary religious movements are very evangelistic, seeking to make converts of everyone who will listen. This series is intended to help the Christian respond to those advances by providing him with information about the cult, comparing the teachings with the Christian faith, and suggesting ways to share the Gospel of Jesus Christ as Savior and Lord. It is hoped that this response can always be in the spirit of the words of St. Peter who said, "always be ready to answer anyone who asks you to explain the hope you have, but be gentle and respectful" (1 Peter 3:15, Beck).

> Erwin J. Kolb
> The Board for Evangelism
> The Lutheran Church—Missouri Synod

Editor's Preface

The Rev. Philip H. Lochhaas is a 1948 graduate of Concordia Seminary, St. Louis, Mo., presently serving The Lutheran Church—Missouri Synod as executive secretary of the Commission on Organizations. In that capacity Rev. Lochhaas receives more than 12,000 inquiries annually concerning various religious organizations. In recent years more than half of these inquiries have requested information on "new religions," both those calling themselves "Christian" and Western expressions of Eastern religions.

In addition to the above responsibilities Rev. Lochhaas has lectured widely and written many articles on various religious movements and organizations.

Coupled with his experience and expertise in the area of religious movements and organizations, Rev. Lochhaas served for 17 years as a missionary-at-large and parish pastor in Oklahoma.

In this booklet Rev. Lochhaas not only explains several of the "New 'Christian' Religions" but provides the reader with background information on the conditions in society in which these religions take root and grow. He also lists some common characteristics ("marks") of the new religions. After describing the teachings and development of several "new religions," Rev. Lochhaas provides his readers with evaluations of the religions, based and founded in the teachings of God's Word. The section on how to respond to people caught up in the "New Religions" is most helpful and practical for the parishioner, parent, and pastor.

David W. Hoover
Board for Missions
Secretary for Mission Support Services
The Lutheran Church—Missouri Synod

Contents

Introduction   8
1. Some General Observations   10
2. Varieties of Experience   16
3. The Unification Church   20
4. The Way International   24
5. The Christian Response   28
   Bibliography   32

Introduction

It began in the 1960s—a restlessness across America, a growing discontent with things as they were. The country was engaged in an unpopular war. It seemed as if little or no progress was being made in solving problems of racial prejudice, poverty, and abuses of civil rights. For too long a large proportion of American society had coasted along comfortably on the prosperity that followed the Second World War. An apathy had developed—the kind of apathy that neither acknowledges nor cares that problems exist. A few political and social leaders began to cry out for more citizen involvement in solving the injustices and inequities in society. Their cries were unheard, for the most part, except by the youth of the land. With their natural idealism and optimism, young people on many college campuses responded to the call for involvement. They gave their support to "activist" aspirants for political office but, more often than not, to no avail.

By the early 1970s a new kind of apathy began showing itself. It wasn't because nothing was being done about the problems in society, but rather because things were being done so slowly. Disenchantment with society led many youth to "drop out," disengage themselves from society. First the Flower Children appeared. These were generally gentle and loving young people who, because of repeated frustrations in their attempts to right the wrongs in society, surrendered to peaceful non-involvement in a world of their own making. That world, however, was quickly invaded by others who wanted to lash out at those in society who disdained the life-style of the Flower Children. The solution to society's problems, they said, was destruction of society and its institutions. The New Left was born. No part of the "System" escaped the wrath of the New Left. The family, the church, the school, industry, and the government were all condemned as exploitive and corrupt. The New Left offered no solutions; it simply took for granted that a better civilization would automatically arise, phoenixlike, from the ashes of the old. Often flaunting sexual irresponsibility and fortified by drugs, some leaders of the New Left promoted deeds of violence that left a trail of wrecked lives and property.

There were, however, some farsighted leaders of youth who saw the "dead end" toward which the New Left was moving. Slowly at first, and then with increasing momentum, they began to gather young people to study the spiritual aspects of society's problems. The Jesus Movement was under way. Whole blocs of young people converted from other movements to the Jesus Movement. "Being high on Jesus" began to replace being high on drugs.

The history of religious revivals in America records how those movements which grew quickly without sending down roots also burned out quickly. Were it not for a few dedicated leaders, the Jesus Movement might have disintegrated as did other movements. Many expressions of the Jesus Movement were indeed shallow and simplistic. "Believe in Jesus" was the solution to every problem, with little application of God-given skills and talents to those problems. In some segments of the Jesus Movement, faith-healing and tongue-speaking received the greatest amount of emphasis. In others, the promise of Jesus' imminent return to earth led to a new kind of "dropping out"—to wait for His arrival. There was no need to plan for any future on earth. Jesus was expected to come before the Jesus People ever reached adulthood. Largely through the efforts of such leaders as Don Williams, David Wilkerson, Larry Norman, and Bill Squires, and others like them, some expressions of the Jesus Movement did become rooted in the Scripture and in "the whole counsel of God." These expressions of the Movement have endured and may affect America's religious life in a positive way for many decades to come.

It should be noted that the most simplistic elements of the Jesus Movement inadvertently may have contributed to the interest in Satanism and the Occult that grew concurrently with the Jesus Movement. Offering mystery, ritual, involvement and application to life, the Occult had an attraction for those youths who never really encountered the true Jesus in the Jesus Movement.

The "new 'Christian' religions" that are so much in evidence today in America also claim to offer the involvement and mystery that were lacking in some expressions of the Jesus Movement. In some cases these new religions involve themselves in occult practices. In others they simply attempt to "supply 'roots' that were lacking in portions of the Movement." In either case, the "new 'Christian' religions" can be seen partially as an outgrowth of the shallower elements of the Jesus Movement and partially as the result of the same conditions in society that gave rise to the Flower Children and the New Left.

Some religious leaders are already looking down the road to see what kind of movement will follow on the heels of the "new 'Christian' religions." It is suspected that there will be a "New Unbelief"—a kind of do-it-yourself humanism that is being inspired and given impetus by the many self-therapy books that are flooding the market.

Regardless of what may follow the "new 'Christian' religions," they give every evidence of remaining a permanent part of America's religious culture. Some of them have already begun to assume the shape of institutionalized churches, with national officers, colleges, and seminaries of their own, and formalized statements of their beliefs. Among these are the Holy Spirit Association for the Unification of World Christianity (the Unification Church) of Sun Myung Moon, and The Way International of Victor Paul Wierwille. Others of the "new 'Christian' religions" are somewhat nomadic groups that are loosely organized, such as the Children of God, "The Church," and hundreds upon hundreds of others.

1

Some General Observations

In this study, the word "religions" is given preference over the word "cults," since the latter is a much abused word today. In popular usage, a "cult" denotes any religious group that differs significantly in faith or practice from that which is considered a "normal" expression of religion in the total culture. The word, however, is sometimes used as a synonym for "denomination" or "sect," especially when referring to a division of a non-Christian religion. A "religion," on the other hand, is a system of faith and practice that is distinct in itself and is not a division of any other religious entity. It is the contention of the author that the "new 'Christian' religions" differ so significantly from what is generally regarded as "Christian" that they are a distinct category in themselves and do not participate, even marginally, in any parent faith.

Are They Really "New"?

Solomon, a thousand years before the birth of Christ, observed that "there is no new thing under the sun" (Eccl. 1:9). He asked, "Is there anything whereof it may be said, See, this is new? It hath already been of old time, which was before us" (v. 10). Solomon's words have a particular application to new doctrines and philosophies that arise from time to time. Throughout the Old Testament there were warnings given against departure from the Word of God. False prophets were to be recognized and severely dealt with. In the New Testament, Jesus also warned against false teachers, especially those who taught falsely in His name or, worse, claimed to be the Christ. *The Living Bible* paraphrases the words of Jesus in Matt. 24:23-24 in an especially succinct manner, "If anyone tells you, 'The Messiah has arrived at such and such a place, or has appeared here or there,' don't believe it. For false Christs shall arise, and false prophets, and will do wonderful miracles, so that if it were possible, even God's chosen ones would be deceived." Elsewhere in the New Testament stern warnings are directed against false prophets because of their distortion of the Word of God by imposing human ideas and interpretations upon it (2 Peter 2:1-3).

It has been proverbial that there have been no new ideas or philosophies for the past thousand years or more—only new appearances of "what hath already been of old time." The "new 'Christian' religions" are not really "new" in their essential differences from historic, orthodox Christianity. Some teachers claim to have received new "revelations" and their interpretations of the Word may appear "new" and strange to Christians who are accustomed to letting Scripture interpret Scripture, but most of that which is "new" has already been addressed by the great creedal confessions of the Christian church, especially the Nicene and Athanasian Creeds. If there is anything new about them, it is their proliferation and their impact upon religious life in America. Many of them will undoubtedly pass from the scene as quickly as they arose, but some will endure and continue to grow. All are likely to leave behind a measure of confusion and disappointment that may compare to the "burnt-over" areas left by former "new" religious movements.

Are They Great in Number?

How widespread are the "new religions"? There are approximately 60 million people in the United States between the ages of 18 and 26. Hardcore members of the new religions probably number about one percent of this age group. Few reliable statistics are available. However, if just one percent of this age group does anything, 600,000 young people are involved. That's an impressive number! Hangers-on and inquirers at any given time may raise the figures to as much as two or three percent. In some geographic areas the number may reach as high as four percent. These are not percentages of which "national calamities" are made, but for parents or loved ones of those caught up in strange religions, the figure might just as well be 100 percent. When the embracing of a new religion involves denial of the deity of Jesus Christ and the all-sufficiency of His atonement, it is a crushing blow to Christian parents.

A word of caution, however, is in place. Literature of the Spiritual Counterfeits Project based in Berkeley, Calif., points out that the rise and growth of new religions must not be permitted to diminish awareness that there are also other forces hostile to the Christian faith. One example may be teenage alcoholism—which affects far more young people than do the new religions. Satan is quite content to suffer the unmasking of certain of his wiles if, in the unmasking, attention is diverted from others of them.

Fertile Ground for New Religions

Before examining the teachings of some of the "new 'Christian' religions," it is helpful to review the *conditions in society* in which these religions take root and grow. This subject is dealt with in depth in the "foundation book" of the Response Series, *How to Respond to ... the Cults* (available from Concordia Publishing House). Here they are noted as they apply in particular to the most recent religious movements. It should be emphasized that the societal conditions that are fertile ground for the growth of the "new 'Christian' religions" are the *same* conditons in which grew the Flower Children, the New Left, the Jesus Movement, and interest in the Occult. It was not due to *changing* conditions that one movement followed another, but the *failure* of each movement in turn to cope with conditions.

There is probably no word used more often to describe how today's individual in society feels than the word "lonely." Alienation has been called the "hallmark of the Seventies." Rapid population growth plus frequent family relocations discourage the building of community. Individuals are forced to be more dependent upon themselves and less upon others. Charles Colson in his frequent public appearances points to alienation as one of the forces responsible for Watergate. Individuals who are lonely often become concerned about only those things that promote their own benefit. Because there seems to be no other choice, selfishness eventually becomes a virtue—and books such as *Looking Out for # 1* remain for months on the best-seller list. "Rights" become more important than privileges, and "freedom" replaces responsibilities.

It is but a short step from dependence upon self alone to worship of self. Slogans become the new moral code: "If you are to find any happiness in life, YOU must create it for yourself!" "If it feels good, DO IT!" "You only go 'round once in life, so live it with all the gusto you can!"

Because individuals are fearful of forming bonds lest these be too soon broken, it becomes easy to remain aloof and add new slogans: All institutions are corrupt! (There has been enough corruption uncovered to make this seem likely!) There are no heroes or heroines; everyone has feet of clay! (Exposés sell magazines!) There are no absolutes; everything is relative! Science can place a man on the moon but cannot solve the simple problems of an earthbound society! The future offers no opportunities— education is wasted! And finally, church members don't act like Christians!

The above is an exaggerated picture of conditions in society. Older folk sometimes have difficulty understanding why young people may think of society in such bleak terms. They forget that our present society was not shaped overnight; it came about gradually. Parents born prior to the Second World War absorbed the changes a little at a time. They were able to adapt to changes because they still retained what Alvin Toffler calls "stability zones"—their life-style, their work, their education and their faith. For the young, however, few of these stability zones were given opportunity to develop. They have not known any society different from the one in which they move. It was thrust upon them full blown.

Those Most Affected by the New Religions

It must be recognized, first of all, that the majority of young people today *can* cope quite well with the bleak conditions they see in society. Most young people can adjust quickly to circumstances. Most are optimistic and serious about their education. Many are quietly religious and have moral values equivalent to those of their parents. Many find their strength and their stability in their Christian faith. Some who are "coping" may suffer from recurrent depression, "the disease (note: disease) of the Seventies," but these, too, often are able to build stability zones in their Christian faith and their Christian families.

A minority of young people will always be found who attempt to escape "coping" by dropping out of society and turning to drugs and sexual adventure. There are others who try every new "therapy" that offers itself, rushing from one healer to another, hoping that this time "this is it!" Their lives are a never-ending "search for something else."

The new religions are most attractive to young people when they are approached at some critical juncture in their lives. In some cases it might be that the youth is despairing, having "tried every trip" without finding a goal or purpose in life. In most cases, however, those who are wooed and won by the new religions are especially wholesome young people, average to above-average students, serious about the future. They generally were involved in sports and had a happy social life in school. For many, the homes in which they were raised were "ideal" as far as family relationships were concerned. But they may be away from their home for the first time in their lives—lonely on a college campus or friendless in a city to which they have gone for employment. It may be that there is a "lull" in their lives, such as the time between graduation and the beginning of a career. There may have been some deep disappointment such as the loss of a close friend, the betrayal by a former ally, or simply a family move to new and strange surroundings.

The new religions, however, appear to be most successful in winning converts from among young people who, as part of their maturing process, are a bit panicky about what direction their lives should take. At such times there seem to be no answers to questions such as: Am I really worth anything to anybody? What goals should I have? How can I tell what is right and what is wrong? How can I choose from all the options there are in life? All too often when they have asked these questions aloud, they have been told by parents and counselors, and even pastors, "No one can answer for you. You have to find your own way, make up your own mind—or the answers won't really be your own." Now, suppose that at this critical juncture in their lives they are told by someone who has made it a point to befriend them, someone who is especially warm and attentive to them, "I used to be all confused. But I have found the answer to all my questions. I found someone who is willing to take responsibility for my choices, willing to focus the direction of my life and involve me in worthwhile projects. Come, and at least meet my friends. . . ."

Some Marks of New Religions

Because there is such a large variety of "new 'Christian' religions" appearing on the religious scene, it is not possible to draw up any sure set of "marks" by which they may be identified. The one sure test is to compare their teachings and practices with the revealed Word of God, the Bible. There are, however, some features that are found in the majority of them, and others that are found in only a few. It is in the display of one or more of these "marks" that a religious entity invites careful scrutiny before any support is given to it.

Almost without exception, each of the "new 'Christian' religions" is headed by one man, a strong, decisive father-figure who supplies the authority in their lives that so many young people subconsciously desire. He may claim to have received a direct commission from God, and he may insist that God speaks to him in an audible voice. Against such direct "revelations" he will permit no contradiction, for who dares to question "what God has spoken"? He may promise to reveal "hidden truths" to his followers, thus assuring them that they are part of the "in-group." The "in-group" feeling is very important, for it can be used to build strong commitment to the group—the one mark that all of the "new religions" display.

For the uninitiated, the teachings of some of the "new 'Christian' religions" can be very difficult to sort out. Some of the leaders assign new meanings to familiar Christian words and phrases—to the point that the uninstructed may despair in the effort to determine what is really taught. "Grace," for example, may be used to mean nothing more than man's "will to believe," and "faith" just another word to signify obedience to the leader. Great emphasis may be placed on comparatively minor matters such as the date of Jesus' birth or the date of Easter. The disciple is thus impressed with the leader's "insights," and there may also be the side-effect of creating doubts in the disciple's mind concerning former teachers who did not "reveal" this "truth."

Most of the new religions are rigidly "moral," although in some of them the moral code may be concerned with only a few external values chosen by the leader for easy compliance lest the followers become discouraged. Often there is no real sense of sin or of salvation. "Salvation" might be thought of as belonging to the group and "sin" as being outside the group, involved in the "profane" world of industry, education, or government. Sometimes the "proof-text" method of Bible study is employed in order to tie the teachings of the group to Christianity. The honest inquirer cannot afford to accept such passages without checking carefully their context in the Scripture and their relationship to the "whole counsel of God" as revealed in the Bible.

Some of the new religious groups seek to support themselves by direct solicitation of funds in public places, and others rely upon the sale of small articles for support. A few charge their own members established fees for their instruction courses, at the same time laying heavy emphasis upon tithing and exceeding the tithe. Occasionally, groups are found that demand that all the material possessions of their followers be signed over to the leaders. There are also among the "new 'Christian' religions" some groups that welcome persecution as "evidence" that they are sole possessors of the "truth."

Again it must be emphasized that not all the new religions bear the same marks. A person must be cautious not to generalize. Careful investigation of each specific group is necessary. Above all, however, each group must be weighed against the Scriptures. What do they teach concerning the deity of Christ, the all-sufficiency of His atonement, the authority and completeness of the Scripture, the fallibility of human leaders?

A "Most Important Paragraph"

The question is frequently asked by distraught parents and Christian church leaders: How could anyone who has studied the Bible believe some of the things that are taught in the "new 'Christian' religions"? The following paragraph is of utmost importance in answering that question:

If the testimony of members and former members of the new religious groups is to be trusted (and there is no good reason to doubt it), few, if any, converts to the new religions were attracted by the *teachings* of those religions. Almost without exception, converts were not aware of what was taught until after they were settled into the group. Even then, in many cases, months went by before they were able to explain to someone else exactly what was taught them. By that time they had identified themselves so closely with the leader and other members of the group that they found no difficulty in accepting what was taught them. That which had attracted them to the group in the first place was the warmth and friendliness they saw and felt—plus the promise of solutions to their problems, of freedom to "be themselves," and the importance and attention that were assigned to them as individuals. Added to all this was the offer of a meaningful life through involvement in "worthwhile projects" and the opportunity to "extend the fellowship" by participation in recruitment programs.

Because the teachings of the "new 'Christian' religions" have not been given the wide exposure that is given their public programs, solicitations, and recruitment drives, the following chapters will explore some of the less formally organized groups, following these with a study of the basic teachings of the more formal "institutionalized" churches such as the Unification Church and The Way International.

Every attempt is being made to set forth honestly and objectively what is taught and there is no intent to malign any group. Information has been gathered from the published writings of the various groups and from interviews with members and former members. In a few cases, reference is made to news reports and journal articles. In *evaluating* the theology of the new religions, however, the perspective of historical, confessional Lutheranism is employed. The Lutheran theological persuasion of the author will be evident, but the primary concerns expressed by him are shared by most of the historic Christian churches.

In the final chapter, suggestions will be made concerning how the Christian must, by his response to the needs of youth and his ministry to members of the new religions and their families, "give an answer to every man that asketh a reason of the hope" that is in him (1 Peter 3:15).

2

Varieties of Experience

There are thousands of religious groups, ranging from large to very small, that declare themselves to be the only true representatives of Christianity in the modern world. Some of these attempt to combine Christianity with eastern religions. They are described, together with others, in the booklet in this series, *How to Respond to . . . the Eastern Religions* (available from Concordia Publishing House). Others offer variations of traditional Christian doctrines shaped by "revelations" that their leaders claim to have received from God. Only a handful of these are nationally known. The rest are of concern to confessional Christians primarily in the limited geographic areas in which they recruit members.

Many of the new religious groups have published no literature because they are always accompanied by their leaders who pass on to them orally the "revelations" they receive. What little information is available comes from former members of these groups who, understandably, are often quite subjective in describing their experiences.

Many of the "new 'Christian' religions" incorporate some kind of communal living into their life-style. Some are nomadic, always wandering from place to place. They often spend the major portion of each day in memorizing Bible portions and preparing answers to give to inquirers from outside their membership. The remainder of the time may be spent in recruitment and soliciting forays into nearby communities.

Members of some of these groups wear long robes at all times, while others are more hesitant to reveal their identity. For some, "God's provender" is discarded food "gleaned" from trash bins behind restaurants and supermarkets. These wear proudly the nickname "garbage-eaters" that has been pinned on them.

One of the most frequently heard complaints from former members of many of these groups concerns the absolute authority of the leaders. The leader alone may make decisions. His commands must not be ignored or contradicted. Furthermore, former members charge that some of the leaders spend only their daylight hours with the disciples and retire at night to quarters more opulent than the camp site. Some former members of some groups have initiated legal action against the leaders in an attempt to recover possessions that they were pressured into signing over. Various descriptions are given of leaders who engaged in occult practices, pronouncing spells and curses upon their adversaries. Others are said to emphasize speaking in tongues and the exorcism of demons. By many of the groups, all non-members are considered eternally lost and are to be shunned—even hated, if they happen to be family members who object to the group. Some former members insist that they were forcibly detained in their first, unsuccessful attempts to leave the group. Experiences, it seems, vary as widely as the names of the groups and the geographic areas in which they are found.

Many of the "new 'Christian' religions" have received unfavorable publicity in newspaper articles and religious journals, as well as in speaking engagements of former members who feel compelled to warn others. Among the groups that appear in news reports from time to time are The Church (or The Body of Christ, or Christian Ministries, Inc.) led by Jim Roberts, sometimes called "Brother Evangelist;" The Church of Bible Understanding (formerly The Forever Family); The Church of the Living Word (or The Walk) headed by John Robert Stevens; a group led by Brother Rama Behera; and hundreds more.

From the perspective of confessional Christian theology, life-style follows belief, practice is shaped by doctrine. The Christian life is a response to God's own love and mercy in Jesus Christ. This is clearly taught in reference to God's promise of a Messiah in the Old Testament and is repeated in every book of the New Testament. The Epistle to the Romans, for example, in its first eleven chapters proclaims powerfully the grace of God in Jesus Christ. It is God who saves, God who declares man justified because of the death of Jesus Christ for the sins of the world, God who reveals His saving grace in the Gospel, and, finally, God who gives man the gift of faith to receive His grace. Then, in chapters twelve and following, the Epistle to the Romans describes the Christian's response to God's great love in Jesus Christ: "I appeal to you, therefore, brethren, *by the mercies of God,* to present your bodies as a living sacrifice, holy and acceptable to God, which is your spiritual worship . . ." (Rom. 12:1 ff.).

There are, in summary, two areas of departure from Scriptural doctrine that have been noted in the "new 'Christian' religions" by observers who are concerned with maintaining the truth of the Gospel. Both are related to the central message of the Scriptures, namely, justification by faith through the grace of God in Jesus Christ. The first area of departure consists of adding to the Scriptures "new revelations" that are claimed to have been received from God Himself. God is said to have spoken either through an audible voice or by means of special "insights" that He has given to the leader alone. The Bible voices stern warnings against teachers who claim to have been commissioned by God to speak that which God Himself has not spoken in His Word. See Jeremiah 23:31 and following for God's own judgment upon prophets who "use their tongue and say, He [God] saith . . .". The apostle Paul, by divine inspiration, pronounces a solemn curse upon anyone who would "pervert the Gospel of Christ" by adding "a different gospel" (Gal. 1:6-9). The second area of departure is related to the first and consists of adding to the Gospel, or replacing it with, unconditional obedience to a human leader. Such obedience may take the form of a specific life-style or a list of duties that must be performed. The apostle Paul did not "yield . . . even for a moment" to anyone who contaminated the pure Gospel of God's saving grace with any form of work-righteousness, (Gal. 2:4-5). The introduction of unconditional spiritual obedience to a human leader strips the Gospel of its love, beauty, joy, and peace and is a denial of the saving grace of God in Jesus Christ.

Among the loosely organized new religions, there is one that is not typical, in that it has published thousands of pages of literature, has granted interviews to news reporters and has perhaps suffered more defections than any other. The "Children of God," nevertheless, are an example of the extremes to which a religious group can go, if it vests its leader with divine authority and follows his commands in every respect.

17

The Children of God

David Brandt Berg (also known as Moses David Berg, King David, or simply "Mo") is the founder and head of the Children of God. His strange odyssey from Christian and Missionary Alliance minister to head of more than one hundred communes ("colonies") of Children of God in sixty-five countries began with his dismissal from his pastorate in Arizona. It is reported that in that moment his hatred for the established church was born. It rapidly grew into hatred for all established institutions—a hatred that shaped much of the theology he began to teach.

David Berg does not hesitate to take credit for originating the Jesus Movement, a claim that is disputed by historians of the Movement. He did operate a teen coffeehouse in Huntington Beach, Calif., for a time, after a brief stint as Public Relations assistant to radio-evangelist Fred Jordan. By means of the coffeehouse Berg built a small following of dedicated disciples. In 1969, when Berg alleges that he "received a prophecy" that California was about to fall into the ocean, he and about a hundred of his disciples took the name "Children of God" and began wandering from place to place. The Children received a sizable boost in membership when three prominent Jesus Movement leaders and some of their disciples joined them. (Since that time all three have disassociated themselves from the Children of God).

In the early days of their existence the Children of God used every opportunity to demonstrate their hatred of "the System." They became notorious for their use of profanity and vulgar language in public places and for their "hymns" damning all churches and all parents. Newspapers reported how they disrupted church services and how they required their converts to turn over their possessions to their leaders as part of "forsaking all,"—possessions, parents, education, jobs, and churches.

While the Children were forbidden to work (except in the communes), they did not shrink from badgering businessmen to support them with money and supplies—while at the same time raging against all business and industry as satanic and responsible for the impending destruction of America. Their continual harping upon the imminent destruction of all but themselves led to their being called "doomsday prophets."

By 1972 there were more than sixty colonies of Children of God in the United States. A great deal of opposition had formed to the Children, and parents were forming organizations that charged the Children with kidnaping, mind-control, holding converts against their will, sexual abuse, and enslavement. As part of their "strategy of survival against persecution," some of the leadership of the Children of God went underground and Berg himself left the country. Since that time, many of the hard-core members have also left the United States. At one time Berg was personally known to all his followers. Today he is seen by very few of them. He does, however, keep in touch with all his colonies by means of his regular "MO Letters" which are sent to them. Some five hundred "MO Letters" have been issued. Some are intended for public sale on the streets; others are addressed to "disciples only." It is in the "MO Letters" that "Moses" David Berg communicates the alleged "revelations" he claims to receive from God. It is in the "MO Letters" that Berg's "theology" is set forth.

Both the Christian and the non-Christian world have attacked the

18

Children of God because of their life-style and suspected mind-control. It is, however, the teachings of David Berg that are responsible for the life-style. The Children of God look upon him as God's chosen prophet for this age, and they are convinced that he receives regular divine revelations and that he alone can lead them to safety in a world that is soon to be destroyed.

Berg's "theology" consists mainly of prophecy and commandments. One might look long and hard at the literature of the Children of God and not find any explicit references to Jesus Christ and His saving work. In the field of prophecy, Berg has been notably unsuccessful. Not only did California fail to slide into the sea, but his prophecy of the comet Kohoutek striking America failed as well. A third prophecy concerning the destruction of America during her bicentennial year also failed. Former members declare that in recent years Berg has gotten more and more involved in spiritism and necromancy in his attempts to predict the future.

Berg's success with the commandments he issues has, however, been spectacular. He is obeyed without question. These instructions, given in recent Mo Letters, increasingly have encouraged sexual promiscuity among the Children of God. By 1976 the Mo Letters were instructing female disciples how to serve as religious prostitutes in order to "hook" more followers for Jesus. This was called "The Flirty Fish Ministry." News magazines, reporting from foreign countries where most of the hard-core Children have gone, suggest that the Children of God have become little more than a crude sex-cult that may be on the verge of collapse because of jealousies and rivalries among the leaders. Mo Letters of recent date, however, claim that the Children are prospering and enjoying "the most explosive growth of a brand-new religious movement in history."

In America and Great Britain the Children of God are not the significant religious attraction for young people that they once were. Some colonies remain and in a few areas recruiting is achieving limited success. According to news reports, the Children of God are concentrating their recruitment efforts upon central Europe and South America.

The effects of the Children of God in America may be around for a long time. There are unknown numbers of youth who are in a state of confusion because of what they were taught in the Children of God. Some of them believe that they "cannot go home," that is, they are convinced that they have made an irreparable break with their families and friends and cannot resume "normal" life. Others are fearful of committing themselves to any cause, lest another disenchantment follow.

Most of the excesses of the Children of God have been avoided by others of the "doomsday prophets." The Children of God, however, serve as an illustration of what can happen when authority is vested in one man, and the "revelations" that he allegedly receives are superimposed upon the Holy Scripture.

In contrast to the nomadic, anti-Establishment life-style of the Children of God, others of the "new 'Christian' religions" are more systematic in their theology and less "separate" from society. Some of these appear to be well on their way toward becoming established churches. Two of the most prominent are considered in the next chapters.

3

The Unification Church

When the Reverend Sun Myung Moon first came to the attention of people outside Korea, it was because he announced that he had been especially chosen by God to lead Christendom in an all-out struggle against world communism. Since that time, however, it has become even more obvious that Moon sees himself also as the bearer of "a new revelation of the truth" for present and future generations. In order to make known this "new revelation," the Unification Church (officially, The Holy Spirit Association for the Unification of World Christianity) has established a theological seminary in the United States, adopted a set of theological affirmations, and is engaged in an aggressive missionary effort. It has also applied for membership in various councils of Christian churches. From the perspective of historic, Biblical Christianity, however, it appears that the Reverend Moon's so-called "Christianity" is far different from that which other churches call "Christian."

Opposition to the Unification Church has come from many quarters. Politically, it has been accused of being in alliance with South Korea's ruling party. Ecclesiastically, it has been denied membership in some Christian church councils on the grounds that it is not Christian. Widespread opposition has come from parents who charge that Moon and his assistants use "mind-control" to alienate young people from their families.

Since the Unification Church claims to exist for the purpose of unifying world *Christianity*, there are questions that must be asked: What is the Unification Church's attitude toward the Bible? What does it teach concerning the person and work of Jesus Christ? And, what of grace, faith, and the Kingdom of God?

Sun Myung Moon and the Bible

Moon's teachings contain much traditional Oriental religious thought, especially the belief that God in His creative activities works through two powers, the masculine and the feminine, the positive and the negative. A brochure distributed by the followers of Moon, *Unification Church: Who We Are,* declares:

> God may be Infinite Mind, the Ground of Being, the Tao—an abstract energizing Force, as represented, for example, by Eastern philosophy, but He is above all, the loving Parent, the Origin and Essence of love, as Christianity declares.

Moon's instruction courses quote the Bible extensively. The Bible is seen as depicting man's predicament. Rescue from that predicament, however, must come from both the Bible and "new revelations of truth," according to Moon. An *Official Statement,* placed as paid advertising in various newspapers, declares that the Unification Church is "based on *a new revelation from God given through Reverend Moon* to prepare the world for the return of Christ" (emphasis added). Much of this "new revelation" is published in the Unification Church's scripture, *The Divine Principle* and in *The Divine Principle Study Guide.*

The Fall of Man

Moon teaches that God created Adam and Eve, but in *The Study Guide* it is stated that they were in an "unstable, unperfected state" when they were first brought together. They were "living together as brother and sister, not as husband and wife." If they had not been approached by Lucifer during this period of "unperfection," the Fall would never have taken place.

Moon's explanation of the Fall is as follows: Lucifer the Archangel had been created by God as a *servant,* whereas Adam and Eve were created as *children* of God. Lucifer naturally assumed that God would love His *children* more than His *servant.* Lucifer was, therefore, jealous of Adam on two counts—Adam was a *child* of God and he was destined to be Eve's husband when he reached maturity. In addition, Eve was feminine and desirable and had somewhat of an admiration for Lucifer, for it seemed to her that Lucifer knew God more intimately than "unperfected" Adam. Lucifer, hoping to take over Adam's position as a *child* of God and husband of Eve, seduced Eve.

The adultery of Lucifer and Eve, Moon declares, was the *spiritual* Fall of mankind. Eve nevertheless hoped that she could rid herself of guilt and regain her position before God, so she tempted Adam to behave as her husband, even though this was premature because of his "unperfection." The union of Adam and Eve was the *physical* Fall of mankind.

The twofold Fall—spiritual and physical—is a basic tenet of the Unification Church and fundamental to its other teachings.

Redemption

According to *The Study Guide,* God did not abandon His children to live in their fallen state. He sent many prophets and teachers, but none of them were able to make complete restoration of perfection. Finally, God sent Jesus as "the Second Adam." According to Moon, Jesus was to redeem man spiritually and physically. His purpose, "to establish the kingdom of God on earth," was not fully accomplished. Through no fault of His own, Jesus failed to make full restoration because the people of His day "aborted his mission" by killing Him before He could complete the task. His death on the cross, though unplanned by God, was still sufficient to redeem man spiritually, but the physical redemption did not occur. That which remained undone was the plan of God for Jesus to take a perfect bride, an embodiment of the Holy Spirit, and beget a new and physically perfect race that was free from the stain of Satan's blood.

In *The Divine Principle,* Moon writes, "Jesus failed in his christly mission; his death on the cross was not an essential part of God's plan for redeeming sinful men." He also writes, "Jesus was not the unique, only begotten Son of God who was pre-existent with the Father before all created things. Jesus attained deity as a man who fulfilled the purpose of creation but can by no means be considered God Himself." Redemption, according to Moon, must be completed by another—"the Lord of the Second Advent" (also called "the third Adam," or simply "the Messiah").

The Study Guide declares that the Lord of the Second Advent must take a bride and form the restored first family of God. He will show all people the truth about God and the universe. He will clarify the "fundamental problems of the Bible" and "clearly show the way for universal salvation." He is the central figure that is awaited by all the "world's higher religions," although they may refer to him by different names.

Discipleship

According to *The Study Guide,* the duty of all people over against the Lord of the Second Advent is to believe in him, attend on him, and cooperate with him in his worldwide work of restoring mankind to perfection, physical redemption. The Lord of the Second Advent is said to already walk the earth at this time, although he has not yet been revealed. Some former followers of Moon say that in private he claims to be the Lord of the Second Advent; and he is believed by his disciples to be the Messiah.

From the Historic Christian Perspective

The primary question troubling Bible students about Moon's church is this: In spite of its name, The Holy Spirit Association for the Unification of World Christianity, can the Unification Church be considered even remotely Christian when it pronounces the *Christ's* atonement insufficient for mankind's full redemption?

From the Scriptural perspective, it is unthinkable that anyone should say that Jesus failed to accomplish His mission because He did not have an opportunity to marry. What Moon says is not an essential part of God's redemption, the crucifixion, is according to Scripture the very act by which God forgives sins and provides full and complete salvation to all who believe. Moon's claim that another, the Lord of the Second Advent, is needed to complete Christ's work brings him under severe Scriptural judgment. The New Testament writers held that their Gospel was complete. St. Paul pronounced a solemn curse upon anyone (including "an angel from heaven") who would presume to offer "another gospel" than the one the apostolic writers proclaimed (Gal. 1:6-9). The inspired writers of the New Testament were especially sensitive to attempts to add conditions to God's gracious offer of salvation in Jesus Christ. Furthermore, in reference to the Lord of the Second Advent, Scripture's stern warnings against future "Christs" are meant to be heeded in every generation (cf. Matt. 24:23-24; 2 Cor. 11:13-15; 1 John 4:1-3). The Scripture also teaches that when the true Christ shall return for His second Advent, He shall not slip into the world unrecognized, to be revealed at first to only a few, but He shall come openly and shall be immediately known to all mankind (Matt. 25:31-32; 2 Thess. 1:7-9, *et al.*).

The National Council of the Churches of Christ in the U. S. A. (the NCC) not only denied membership to the Unification Church, but in the report of its Commission on Faith and Order stated, "The Unification Church is not a Christian Church." Reasons cited, even under the broad definitions and standards of the Council, included, "Its doctrine of the nature of the Triune God is erroneous. . . . Its Christology is incompatible with Christian teaching and belief. . . . Revelations are invoked as divine and normative in *Divine Principle* which contradict the basic elements of the Christian faith. . . . *Divine Principle* recognizes a higher authority (than the Bible) in Sun Myung Moon."

Moon's anti-communism may appeal to many, but anti-communism is not in itself a mark of Christianity. The Christian faith transcends all political systems and casts the "Light of the World" upon all political injustice whether it exists under communism or any other form of government.

Controversy

Controversy seems to have followed the Reverend Moon ever since 1936 when, at the age of 16, he claims to have had a "special revelation" from God that appointed him to a unique ministry of fulfilling God's will in the world. Facts are blurred and reports are contradictory concerning the years that followed—excommunication from Korea's Presbyterian Church, imprisonment by North Korean authorities, charges that led to his arrest by South Korean police.

Controversy has also swirled around Moon's mass weddings (as many as 1,800 couples at one time in a Korean arena), his alleged political involvements, the wealth of the Unification Church, Moon's personal financial holdings, and the tactics used by young "Moonies" who sell candles, peanuts, flowers, and candy on street corners, in shopping centers and from door to door.

Furthermore, controversy has also surrounded projects of the Unification Church that are not always easily recognized as such. "Creative community projects," the International Cultural Foundation, the Collegiate Association for the Research of Principle and the International Conference on the Unity of the Sciences are a few of the more than twenty-five "front organizations" that have been cited by various writers.

Controversy surrounding the Reverend Moon, however, has become most intense in reference to "what he is doing to the minds of his young converts." "Ex-Moonies" have become instrumental in forming organizations (e.g., the International Foundation for Individual Freedom) for the sake of providing information concerning Moon's alleged "brainwashing" of his disciples. They relate remarkably consistent stories of the use of isolation, fatigue, nutritionless diet, peer pressure, and the constant barrage of "propaganda" to break down the independent thinking of the "Moonies." The *Official Statement* of the Unification Church, previously cited, dismisses these allegations as "distortions and misrepresentations" and points to a Superior Court's dismissal of charges of "brainwashing" brought by some parents.

4

The Way International

Founder and head of The Way International is Victor Paul Wierwille. Little is known of him beyond what is revealed in his brief biography at the end of several of his books. It is noted that he studied at the Mission House College and Seminary at Sheboygan, Wis., and at the University of Chicago. He received his master of theology degree from Princeton Theological Seminary, and "later he completed his work for the doctor of theology degree." It is not stated from which school Wierwille received his doctorate. He was ordained into the ministry of the Evangelical and Reformed Church (later, United Church of Christ). In 1953 Wierwille began teaching a "Power for Abundant Living" course. After leaving his denomination, this course grew into The Way Biblical Research Center near New Knoxville, Ohio, the present headquarters and heart of The Way.

By teaching "Biblical research" instead of "religion," Wierwille has built The Way into a youth-oriented movement that reaches into 50 states and several foreign countries. In many respects, The Way appears to be becoming a church body in itself, with centers and colleges being established and an aggressive missionary program. The basic theological position of The Way is set forth in the books written by Wierwille.

The Way and the Bible

The Way holds that the Bible is literally and inerrantly accurate as God gave it to the original writers. The only English translation of the Bible used in The Way is the King James Version. Throughout his books, however, Wierwille frequently inserts his own parenthetic explanations into quotations of the King James text. His understandings are said to be drawn from the Peshitta (Syriac) text and other "eastern texts" that he believes to be the most reliable. By assigning various portions of the Bible (the Old Testament, the Gospels, the Epistles) to different "administrations" (similar to "dispensations" or Bible eras), Wierwille arrives at the Bible's message for Christians of today. In interpreting the sacred text, he calls attention to many "figures of speech."

The Nature of God

The Way totally and unequivocally rejects the doctrine of the Holy Trinity as it is taught in historic Christian theology. Wierwille has written extensively on that subject (Cf. his *Jesus Christ is NOT God*). He uses the terms "God" and "Holy Spirit" synonymously and recognizes no distinction of person between the two (Cf. *Receiving the Holy Spirit Today*, throughout). He does not accept the existence of Jesus prior to His conception in Mary's womb. In *Jesus Christ is NOT God*, Wierwille declares, "In other words, I am saying that Jesus Christ is not God, but the Son of God. They are not 'co-eternal, without beginning or end, and co-equal.' Jesus Christ was not literally with God in the beginning; neither does he have all the assets of God" (p. 5). Wierwille has high praise for Jesus, but denies His deity. He writes that we can speak of Jesus as eternal because the Father knew from eternity that He was going to create Jesus (*The Word's Way,* p. 28). In *Jesus Christ is NOT God,* Wierwille omits reference to John 17:5, one of the clear passages setting forth Jesus' preexistence.

Relative to the Trinitarian formula for Baptism given in Matt. 28:19, Wierwille implies that these words do not belong in the Bible when he writes, "If the command in Matthew 28:19 were truly given, then ten days later Peter had already forgotten what Jesus had told him" (*The Bible Tells Me So,* p. 139).

Man, Holy Spirit, and holy spirit

Man, says Wierwille, is composed of three parts—body, soul and spirit. Wierwille's definition of these words is important because it affects the interpretation of those passages of the Bible that speak of the soul. The body, he says, is simply the body. The soul is the life-principle, the breath-life which plants and animals also possess. Spirit is God's image. When a man dies, the soul ceases to exist, for there is nothing immortal about it (*The Word's Way,* p. 53). When Adam and Eve sinned, he declares, spirit disappeared. They were then just body and soul like the animals (*Power for Abundant Living,* p. 258).

Wierwille makes a sharp distinction between *H*oly Spirit and *h*oly spirit. On the day of Pentecost, he asserts, *h*oly spirit (the image of God) was made available to man as a gift of the *H*oly Spirit (God). In his book, *Receiving the Holy Spirit Today,* Wierwille expands on the distinction between *S*pirit and *s*pirit, describing methods by which man can breathe in the spirit. In the end, the responsibility rests upon man: "He is a son of God by a decision of his will to believe" (p. 238).

Once a believer has received holy spirit, it is assumed that he will give evidence by speaking in tongues. To assist believers in fulfilling this responsibility, Wierwille gives instructions in the technique in *The New, Dynamic Church* (pp. 122—5). He declares that there is only one *gift* given by the Holy Spirit (God); the nine commonly thought of as gifts are "manifestations" of the one gift, holy spirit. In reply to the question why every believer, then, does not display all nine "manifestations," Wierwille explains that it is because he has not willed to display them. "As he will" in 1 Cor. 12:11, he declares, "means 'as each man wills'" (*Receiving the Holy Spirit Today,* p. 179).

Other Doctrines

Baptismal services in The Way do not use water. Baptism with water is rejected as inapplicable to the present "administration": "To say that there is water involved in baptism can only be private interpretation." Wierwille writes. He explains Peter's reference to water in Acts 10:47 as a lapse on Peter's part (*The Bible Tells Me So,* pp. 135—6). He does not make many references to Holy Communion in his books, but does refer to the "great physical healing power in Holy Communion" (p. 86).

Since speaking in tongues is the primary means of communicating with God in The Way, Wierwille does not lay a great deal of emphasis on prayer. He writes, "The Word of God is the Will of God. . . . We need no longer pray the pitiful 'If it be Thy Will.' Only someone unlearned or ignorant of the Word of God will pray 'If it be Thy Will.' The man who knows the Word of God knows what is God's Will' (*The New, Dynamic Church*, p. 236).

Some of the controversy surrounding the writings of Victor Paul Wierwille has to do with less fundamental teachings, but teachings that nevertheless involve Bible interpretation. Wierwille, for example, teaches the following: Mary was a virgin only until Jesus was conceived, not until He was born (*The Word's Way*, p. 168). Four men were crucified with Jesus—two malefactors and two thieves (p. 236). Jesus was buried on a Wednesday and rose on a Saturday (pp. 187 ff.). Jesus did not say on the cross, "My God, My God, why hast Thou forsaken Me?" but words that sound similar to these in Aramaic, "My God, for this purpose was I reserved" (pp. 271—2). Wierwille's interpretation of 1 Cor. 14:34-35 is that it was "the prophets' wives" who were to keep silence in the churches, for they had been "carrying on and thereby degrading their husbands as men of God" (*Receiving the Holy Spirit Today*, pp. 238—9).

An Evaluation

From the historical Christian perspective, the doctrines of The Way are not "new." There are, for example, similarities between the theology of Victor Paul Wierwille and that of Paul of Samosata, a "dynamic monarchianist" who was bishop of Antioch from 260 to 272 A.D. Paul of Samosata taught that God inspired the man Jesus who was then gradually united to God by moral development and "adoption" in a perfect unity of will, but not of substance. Because of His merit, he continued, Jesus was raised from the dead and exalted to a position of divinity, but not of deity. Paul was excommunicated in 269, but managed to hold on to his bishopric for three more years. Paul of Samosata's departure from the theology of the early church was one of the contributory causes for the adoption of the Nicene Creed in 325 A.D.

Across the centuries since the days of the early church, historic confessional Christianity has fully subscribed to the words of the Nicene Creed. In direct answer to theologies such as that of Victor Paul Wierwille, the Nicene Creed states:

> I believe in . . . one Lord Jesus Christ . . . begotten of His Father before all worlds, God of God, Light of Light, Very God of Very God, begotten, not made, being of one substance with the Father, by whom all things were made, who for us and for our salvation came down from heaven . . . whose kingdom shall have no end . . . and I believe in the Holy Ghost . . . who proceedeth from the Father and the Son, who with the Father and the Son together is worshiped and glorified . . . I acknowledge one Baptism for the remission of sins.

From this historical Christian perspective, the theology of The Way is seen as standing in direct contradiction to the most fundamental Christian doctrines—the Trinity, including the deity of Christ and the person of the Holy Spirit; conversion, particularly the Holy Spirit's activity and not "man's will to believe"; and the doctrine of Scripture, including its own rules of interpretation.

The Way has assumed the posture of an interdenominational Biblical research group rather than a church. It is imperative, therefore, that Christian church members be aware of The Way's theological pronouncements. Classes and courses taught by The Way must not be thought of as opportunities for supplementary Bible study for Christians committed to historic confessional theology. The basic incompatibility between The Way's theology and that of the orthodox Christian churches may not be apparent to an inquirer immediately, since The Way uses familiar Christian words and phrases to express its theology. In his book, *Jesus Christ is NOT God,* Wierwille acknowledges, "Many people may be misled because while using the same language or words, we don't mean the same thing" (p. 4).

The object of all Way units is to enroll people in "Power for Abundant Living" courses—usually consisting of twelve three-hour sessions (approximate cost, $85) using textbooks by Wierwille. Way units are particularly active on college campuses.

Unlike many of the "new 'Christian' religions," The Way does not isolate its members from their families and friends nor take them from their schools or jobs. Former members, however, say that there is a strong tendency for Way members to withdraw from former acquaintances who will not accept The Way and to become alienated from their families for the same reason. They also say that while they were members of The Way, they felt "pressured" into transferring to a Way college or giving full time to working for The Way. Late in 1977 some hostility was encountered by The Way in areas where its presence was strongly felt. This is especially true in New Knoxville, Ohio, the location of The Way's headquarters, where Wierwille, on Reformation Sunday, 1977, nailed a proclamation to the door of the United Church of Christ of which he had once been a member. It began, in large letters, "JESUS CHRIST IS NOT GOD— NEVER WAS AND NEVER WILL BE" . . .

5

The Christian Response

The Christian's response to the "new 'Christian' religions" begins with the love of God in Jesus Christ. "God commended His love toward us, in that, while we were yet sinners, Christ died for us" (Rom. 5:8). Through this Gospel the Holy Spirit of God "calls, gathers, enlightens, and sanctifies" the Christian church and "keeps it with Jesus Christ in the one true faith." An identifying mark of the true Christian church is its proclamation of the pure Word of God as it is revealed in the Holy Bible without human addition or alleged new revelations.

Today's proliferation of "new 'Christian' religions" is a challenge to Christian people to be ever more firmly rooted in the Scripture, growing in grace and in the knowledge of the Lord Jesus Christ and giving testimony to that grace with their lips and with their lives. The Christian's response to the "new 'Christian' religions," then, is centered in the Word of God—as it is proclaimed publicly in the church and as Christian witness is given to those who have joined a new religion and to parents or loved ones of those who have joined.

The Church's Public Proclamation

The church's strength lies in her proclamation of that which is lacking in the new religions, namely, proper distinction between Law and Gospel, clear Scriptural concepts of sin and grace, man's need because of his alienation from God and God's gracious supply of this need in Jesus Christ. For Christian pastors this means much careful and prayerful preparation of sermons. It means, for all pastors and teachers, careful use of theological language. It must never be taken for granted that because words are familiar, their meanings are understood. The church must not hesitate or be fearful in speaking Scripture's non-options regarding what constitutes the Christian life. The church must speak with authority of the sufficiency of Christ's redemption and the certainty of God's promise of forgiveness in Jesus Christ. In all the varied facets of the church's ministry, commitment to Christ must be nurtured—not cultlike devotion to a pastor, an organization, or a congregation.

Fathers, mothers, Sunday school teachers, youth, children, church officers—all who confess the name of Jesus—must be challenged to be the people of God, people whose conduct is befitting the Gospel of Christ (Phil. 1:27).

Particularly in reference to its youth program, each congregation ought to regularly and fearlessly analyze whether it is addressing the conditions that are "fertile ground" for the growth of the new religions (see Chap. 1). Do the members of the congregation exhibit warmth and friendship to one another? Are the youth made to feel that they are a vital, valued part of the church? Are they given an opportunity to be participants in worship or must they be spectators only? To what extent are they given opportunities to use their skills and talents in positions of trust in the church? Living as we do in a youth-oriented age, is the congregation adequately staffed with competent, trained leaders to meet the needs of youth? Are there priorities that ought to be re-arranged? Without getting sidetracked into thinking *only* in terms of the new religions, it is imperative that Christian congregations see the youth as the church of *today*, not just the church of tomorrow.

Ministry to Those Who Have Joined a New Religion

No ministry should ever be undertaken without thorough, prayerful preparation. Honesty compels the Christian witness to discount rumors and determine what are the facts regarding the new religion about which he is concerned. Primary sources, if at all possible, should be studied side by side with the Bible. Helpful literature can be purchased at any Christian bookstore. Sound, Gospel-centered materials are published by the Spiritual Counterfeits Project and Intervarsity Christian Press, and many others.

Some "helpful hints" for those who have an opportunity to witness to joiners of a new religion:

1. Approach them with an expectant heart, having committed your witness to the Holy Spirit for His gracious influence.
2. Exhibit a genuine interest in the person to whom you are witnessing. There *are,* indeed, things that you can learn from them about commitment, loyalty, sacrifice, and zeal.
3. Display Christian love and patience, never condescension or "tolerance," for all people are in equal need of God's grace in Jesus Christ.
4. Avoid all hostility, ridicule, argument, "closing the door."
5. Tell in your own words what Jesus means to you. No one can question or "argue" with you about that. Emphasize how Jesus came seeking you— you did not have to win His approval in any way.
6. Let your conduct express your own personal assurance, peace, joy. These are God's gifts to you in the Holy Spirit.

A Ministry to Parents and Loved Ones

To parents and loved ones, the loss of someone to one of the new religions *can be* more traumatic than the death of that person. This may appear to be a gross overstatement, yet it is borne out by experience. When denial of the deity and sufficiency of Jesus Christ is involved, when parents are cursed as "satanic," or when the authority of the Holy Scripture is cast aside in favor of human invention—there appears to be little comfort that can be offered and little that can be done. But there *is* comfort—and there *are* things that can be done:

1. Be assured, God is not dead! Prayer can and does change things. Pray with and for those who suffer heartaches.
2. Parents should not condemn themselves. Remember that a large percentage of those who join the new religions come from stable, even "ideal," homes, insofar as human beings can furnish these. God's Word does not return void. What parents have taught, under the Holy Spirit's guidance, may yet be blessed in ways that cannot be imagined in times of distress.
3. Parents and loved ones should know that they are not alone—there are others like themselves with whom they can exchange ministry and communication of the promises of God.

4. In times of stress, Christians are urged not to be fearful of those who trouble them, but in their hearts to reverence Christ as Lord (1 Peter 3:14-15). In such reverence, Peter calls upon Christians to "always be ready to answer anyone who asks you to explain the hope you have, but be gentle and respectful" (v. 16).

5. Further estrangement of those who have joined a new religion should be avoided. There are three "deadly" attitudes that must not be assumed: (1) Amused tolerance ("It's just a phase they're going through"); (2) Rationalization ("It's at least better than if they were on drugs"); and (3) Defensiveness ("Well, they dress better, are more polite . . .").

6. The door must always be kept open. Some groups hold their disciples by telling them, "You will never be accepted home again." No conditions must be put on love, as "We'll love you if you give up this nonsense and come back home." Now, more than ever before, the youth may need assurance of parental love.

7. Recognize the folly of self-pity. Playing upon a person's emotions or assuming a martyr's role may only cause disgust in a youth who is sincere about his/her new religion. Avoid, "How could you do this to ME?" or "You're just killing your father with this nonsense!"

8. Keep lines of communication open. If the group is one that seeks to hold its converts by removing them to unfamiliar surroundings, all communications, names, addresses, phone numbers, should be retained. It has happened that some have pleaded with their parents, "Come and get me," but were unable to describe their location.

9. Parents should be aware that if the youth returns home, they and/or the youth could, by some groups, be threatened, harassed, put under constant pressure.

10. Money should not be sent. Some groups use every kind of pretense they can invent to get money. (Others are proficient at raising money and ask for none). Medicines or doctor's care, if they are really needed, can often be arranged with direct payments from the parents to the doctor or pharmacist.

11. "Professional deprogrammers" should be avoided. Some operate outside the law and have been overruled by the courts. The tactics employed by some of them are as traumatic as the "brainwashing" of which some groups are accused.

12. Be informed! A person must not assume that what is true, or rumored to be true, of one group is true of all. Some wholesome Bible study groups have been maligned simply because somebody had not heard of them before and assumed that they were "one of the cults."

13. Hear the Word of the Lord: "My God shall supply all your need according to His riches in glory by Christ Jesus" (Phil. 4:19). These words are spoken in reference to the One who has never broken a promise or failed to bless those who put their trust in Him.

In Conclusion

Don't be surprised to find that expressions of concern over the "new 'Christian' religions" are beginning to become unpopular. In an age of easy tolerance, such as the age in which we live, even those most guilty of exploiting others can assume the role of victims of bigoted persecutors, then in the public eye become martyrs, and finally, saints.

The Epistles of the New Testament were written in days not unlike our own as far as attacks on the Gospel of Jesus Christ are concerned. Paul's two Epistles to Timothy, the two Epistles of Peter and 1 John are especially profitable reading in connection with today's "new religions." They warn against those who forsake the Word of God and set themselves up as authorities. Therefore Peter closes his Second Epistle with the words:

> You, beloved, knowing this beforehand, beware lest you be carried away with the error of lawless men and lose your own stability. But grow in the grace and knowledge of our Lord and Savior Jesus Christ. To Him be the glory both now and to the day of eternity. Amen.

Bibliography

Beck, Hubert F., *How to Respond to . . . the Cults* ("Response Series"). St. Louis: Concordia Publishing House, 1977.

Breese, Dave, *Know the Marks of Cults*. Wheaton: SP Publications, 1975.

Cohen, Daniel, *The New Believers* (not from religious perspective). New York: Ballantine Books, 1975.

McBeth, Leon, *Strange New Religions*. Nashville: Broadman Press, 1977.

Petersen, William J., *Those Curious New Cults* (Study Guide also available). New Canaan, Conn.: Keats Publishing, Inc., 1975.

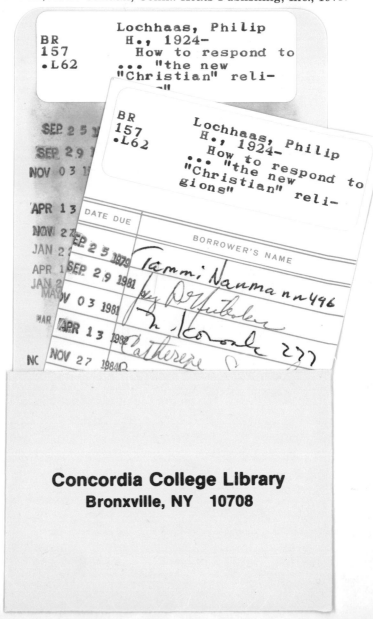

Concordia College Library
Bronxville, NY   10708